The Hat

Jackie Andrews
Illustrated by Betina Ogden

Rigby

A Harcourt Achieve Imprint

www.Rigby.com
1-800-531-5015

Joey saw the mail carrier drive away from their house as he was getting dressed. It was his birthday, and he wondered if there would be any mail for him. He had some cards already, but he wondered if he would receive any packages.

"Package for you, Joey!" his mom called.

Joey sped downstairs with bare feet, forgetting to put on his socks and gym shoes. His mom stood at the bottom, grinning and holding out a brown package covered in labels and stamps.

"Here you are, and it looks as if it's from Grandma," she told him.

"Grandma usually just sends me money for my birthday, not packages," said Joey.

"Maybe this time she found something special she thought you'd like," said his mom.

Joey carried his package into the kitchen and put it on the table as if it were some kind of mysterious treasure.

"Aren't you going to open it?" asked his mom as she handed him a bowl of milk and cereal.

He was a little nervous to open the gift up in front of his mother.

"Um—not just yet because I want to eat my breakfast first, feed the dog, and get ready for school."

What if Joey opened it up in front
of his mother, and it was something
he really didn't like? He would have to
pretend to like it so that his mother would
not be upset.

Besides, he couldn't think of anything
he might possibly want that would fit
that shape.

While he ate his breakfast, he read the comics on the back of the cereal box. He had read them several times that week already, but today it helped take his mind off his package, which still sat unopened on the table.

After he finished his breakfast, fed the dog, and got ready for school, he had no excuses. He opened the package, and inside was something soft wrapped in red tissue paper.

Suddenly he had a horrible feeling that Grandma really had sent him something truly awful, but he unwrapped the tissue paper anyway, and his heart sank.

Inside was a thick, funny-looking knitted
hat. It was all the colors of the rainbow
and was clearly made up of leftover
pieces of chunky yarn, as some of the
colors broke off in odd places. There
were two large puffy, woolly pom-poms
dangling from the top of it.

"Oh, no! What is it?" groaned Joey.

"Oh, look at that. What a nice hat," said his mom. "That hat will keep you as snug as a bug in a rug, Joey."

Ugh! Joey didn't want to be as snug as a bug in a rug.

It was the kind of hat Joey would
never ever want to be seen wearing, and
certainly not in front of his friends.

Joey wondered what made Grandma
send it, as her usual ten-dollar bill would
have been a much more welcome present.
He shook out the wrapping paper.

Nothing more tumbled out—not even a letter. Joey decided that he would have to lose the hat at the first opportunity. He went back upstairs to put on his socks and gym shoes, stuffing the hat with its wrappings in his trash can.

Then he called, "Good-bye, Mom!" and dashed out of the house to meet the school bus. Maybe by the time he got home again, his mom would have emptied the can, and he'd never have to see the hat again.

When Joey told his friend Dan about the peculiar hat, Joey said, "But don't worry because I've taken care of it."

When Joey got home from school, he ran straight upstairs to put his school bag away. He had forgotten about the hat, so he was quite surprised when he saw it sitting on the middle of his bed.

"Oh, no!"

"Joey?" his mom called up the stairs. "I found your special hat in your trash can this morning."

"Oh, I must have put it there with the tissues," Joey said.

"Well, I put it on your bed so that you wouldn't lose it again," his mom said.

"How am I going to get rid of this hat without upsetting my mother?" Joey thought to himself.

When Saturday came, Joey and his mother walked to the movie theater. On the way, he slowly took the hat from his pocket and let it fall onto the sidewalk, whistling, as if nothing had happened.

"Excuse me, young man!"

Joey turned to look.

There was a woman walking a dog and hurrying towards Joey and his mother.

"You dropped your hat," the woman said.

"That was very kind of you to notice," Joey's mother said as she took the hat from the dog's mouth.

"Hmm . . . I wonder how that happened," Joey said sadly, as he took the hat from his mother, stuffing it into his pocket again.

On Sunday morning, Joey remembered there was a sale at the community center near the end of his block. He could leave the hat there!

Joey rode his bike to the community center and gave the hat to one of the women who was walking inside to set up her stand.

"Oh, what a special hat! I'm sure we'll be able to sell it," she said.

Joey left the center feeling much better now that the hat was out of his hands.

Later that day, the hat was lying on the kitchen table.

"Oh, no! Say it isn't so! I thought I lost this," Joey told his mom.

"It was in the community center sale," said his mom, putting a bowl of spaghetti in front of him. "I guess it fell out of your pocket again."

Joey thought, "Am I ever going to be able to get rid of this thing?" Then he had another idea.

On Monday morning, he dropped the hat off at the lost and found at school.

On Monday afternoon, when Joey was in class, Mr. Eastman asked the students to take out the object they were supposed to bring from home.

"Oh, no!" thought Joey. "I was so worried about getting rid of the hat that I forgot my homework. I was supposed to bring an object from home for our plays."

"Where can I find an object from home quickly?" Joey thought to himself. Suddenly he had an idea.

"Mr. Eastman, I think I dropped my object when I came into school this morning, so can I see if someone turned it in to the school secretary?" Joey asked.

Mr. Eastman allowed him to go to the school secretary.

Joey walked as fast as he could to the school secretary.

"I lost a colorful hat this morning," Joey said. "Do you happen to have one in the lost and found?"

Joey looked through the box.

"Here it is!" said Joey excitedly. "I thought I lost it!"

Joey took the hat and went quickly back to class.

As Joey entered his classroom,
Mr. Eastman told him to work with Dan.
They were to write a play using the
objects that Joey and Dan had brought
to school.

Dan giggled when he saw Joey walk
over to him with his colorful hat.

Dan thought it would be good to act out the life of the hat as different people owned it.

"We could start with a grandma knitting it, then giving it to her grandson. He takes it on a trip and loses it," Dan suggested.

"Great idea, Dan," said Joey. They quickly worked out events and characters.

"How are we going to end it?"
Joey asked.

"Since I brought this old flannel shirt,
we could leave the hat on top of a
scarecrow in a field," Dan suggested.

"You could pretend you are the
scarecrow," Joey said.

"Here . . . let me try it on," Dan said
as he took the hat and tried to tug it over
his head.

"It's too small," Dan said.

"Give it to me," Joey said, taking the hat from his friend. Joey pulled at the brim to stretch it, but something seemed to be preventing it from stretching fully. There was an odd crackly sound.

"Hmmm! It looks as if there's something stuck in the hat."

Joey turned the hat over and felt the folded brim. His fingers came to something stiff and papery.

"What is it?" asked Dan.

Joey carefully unfolded the brim and gave the hat a shake. A crumpled piece of paper fell onto the floor, and he bent down and picked it up.

"It's a ten-dollar bill!" Joey shouted as he smoothed it out and stared at it. He thought of his grandma hiding it in the hat, and he began to laugh. He laughed so hard that the rest of the class stopped what they were doing and looked across at him.

"What's so funny, Joey?" asked Mr. Eastman.

Joey told Mr. Eastman the whole story, even how he put the hat in the lost and found box in the morning.

"So your hat was pretty special after all!" said Mr. Eastman with a smile.